Five One Act Plays by Mark Twain

ADAPTED FROM HIS SHORT STORIES

by Jules Tasca

SAMUEL FRENCH, INC.

45 WEST 25TH STREET   NEW YORK 10010

7623 SUNSET BOULEVARD   HOLLYWOOD 90046

LONDON   *TORONTO*

AUTHOR'S NOTE

Mr. Twain's character humor carries itself without elaborate stage designs. The settings may be extremely simple; even the lightning piece may be done with a simple window flat and a makeshift fireplace.

Membranous Croup

CHARACTERS

CAROLINE—A woman in her 30's who is deathly afraid of germs infecting her family. She treats her husband as if he were completely incapable of understanding anything at all, let alone questions of hygiene.

MORTIMER—Caroline's husband. A man in his 30's who will go along with his wife but not agree with her.

PENELOPE—A child of 9 or so years old.

NURSE—A young girl.

DOCTOR—Old country doctor, the type who would get up and come out at night in a surrey.

DESCRIPTION

MEMBRANOUS CROUP—2 males, 2 females, 1 child. Adapted from Mark Twain's humorous battle of the sexes story dealing with the overly protective mother, Caroline and the overly protected Mortimer. Caroline, fearful of a croup epidemic, hears her daughter cough; this sets in motion a whole series of attempts to "cure" her daughter before it's too late. Grumbling Mortimer, of course, has to carry out every order his wife gives including giving medicine to his daughter every 5 minutes, putting 8 blankets on her, turning up the heat, and rubbing the girl's throat with an inch thick layer of goose grease. Caroline is finally squelched at the end when the doctor arrives and declares that this little girl is not ill at all and Mortimer has the last line and the last laugh.

Membranous Croup

(*Time: Turn-of-the-Century. There is a simple curtained window upstage. The stage itself is divided in half by folding chairs or a few simple risers. On one side are two adult beds, on the other a child's bed and a cradle.* MR. MORTIMER MCWILLIAMS *is getting into a nightgown and cap.* CAROLINE MCWILLIAMS, *already in night clothes, turns down her bed. A child,* PENELOPE, *is chewing on some wood as she sits on the floor drawing on some papers.*)

MORTIMER. Darling, I wouldn't let that child be chewing that pine stick if I were you.

CAROLINE. Precious, where's the harm in it?

MORTIMER. Love, it's notorious. Pine. And no nutrition. Worse wood a child can eat.

CAROLINE. Hubby, you know better than that. Doctors all say the turpentine in pine wood is good for weak back and kidneys.

MORTIMER. Penelope's spine and kidneys are affected?

CAROLINE. Who said her kidneys and spine were affected?

MORTIMER. My love, you intimated it.

CAROLINE. The idea. I never intimated anything of the kind.

MORTIMER. Why, my Dear, a minute ago you said—

CAROLINE. I don't care what I said. There isn't any *harm* in the child's chewing pine stick if she wants to,

7

and you know it. And she shall chew it, too. So there now.

MORTIMER. Say no more, Dear. I see your reasoning. I'll order two or three cords of the best fire wood to-day. No child of mine shall want while I—

CAROLINE. Please, just get ready for bed. And let me have some peace. A body can't make the simplist remark but you start arguing and arguing 'till you don't know what you're talking about.

MORTIMER. I see my mistake, Dear. Don't know where I became such a fool.

(*The children's nurse enters the children's room with* PENELOPE's *nightgown*.)

walkin

NURSE. Penelope!
CAROLINE. Your nurse, Penelope.

(*The child runs to her own bedroom and the nurse dresses her in her nightgown*.)

NURSE. (*Yelling into the* McWILLIAMS.) Know what?
MORTIMER. What's the matter?
NURSE. Georgie Gardner has the croup.
CAROLINE. Oh, Mortimer, there's another one. Little Georgie Gardner is taken.
MORTIMER. Membranous croup?
NURSE. Just croup.
CAROLINE. Membranous croup. I know it is. It's going around.
MORTIMER. Any hope for him?
CAROLINE. Oh, what's to become of us?
MORTIMER. Come on, Dear. We have nothing to worry about. We're all in good health.
PENELOPE. (*She runs in from her room as* NURSE

turns down her bed. She kisses her father.) Daddy, goodnight. (*Then she kisses her mother.*) Goodnight, Mamma. ~~half way on~~

NURSE. Come on, Penelope. Time for bed. Say your prayer for mommy and daddy and let's go.

PENELOPE. (*Kneels.*) Now I lay me down to sleep . . . (*She coughs.*)

CAROLINE. (*She springs to her feet and gasps.*) She's got it!

MORTIMER. But . . .

CAROLINE. Don't say another word! She's got it! I want the baby's crib taken in here, Mortimer.

MORTIMER. But Dearest . . .

CAROLINE. Mortimer, I will not say it again. The baby's crib in here.

(MORTIMER *gets out of bed and crosses into the children's room.* CAROLINE *holds* PENELOPE *close and comforts her.*) ~~follow~~

NURSE. What is it?

MORTIMER. She thinks all the germs in the world are having a convention in Penelope. ~~help with or B~~

NURSE. Oh.

PENELOPE. Mamma, I'm all right.

CAROLINE. Don't say another word, Penelope. It only irritates the throat.

MORTIMER. (*He motions for the* NURSE *to help him drag the baby's crib into their room.*) Okay?

CAROLINE. Now Penelope's bed is in there alone should she have another attack.

MORTIMER. Attack?! She coughed.

CAROLINE. Mortimer, should she have another attack, we won't hear her.

MORTIMER. I have a feeling you'd hear her.

CAROLINE. Mortimer.

MORTIMER. What do you want me to do?

CAROLINE. Pull her bed out in the hall.

(NURSE *looks at* MORTIMER. MORTIMER *nods yes. They then proceed to pull* PENELOPE's *bed into the hall.*)

CAROLINE. Germs travel so fast, Penelope. Mortimer, Nurse, do you think we should all move downstairs and leave Penelope up here?

MORTIMER. (*Pause.*) We could move to the county seat until Penelope blows over.

CAROLINE. Do not—do not—try to make light of this, Mortimer. We're moving to the downstairs bedroom.

NURSE. I wouldn't be alarmed, Mam.

CAROLINE. Mortimer, oh, look at the baby.

MORTIMER. Looks like your standard baby to me, but what do I know.

CAROLINE. What can make baby sleep so?

MORTIMER. My Darling, baby always sleeps like a graven image.

CAROLINE. I know. I know. But there's something peculiar about his sleep now. He seems to—to—he seems to breathe so regularly—oh, this is dreadful. You must go for the doctor, Maria. Dead or alive, the doctor must come. Then you stay the night at your own home. Germs.

(NURSE *puts* PENELOPE *in bed and exits.*)

MORTIMER. I don't think that we should've sent her away just because . . .

CAROLINE. Oh, I know it. There's something fright-
ful about this night. I sent her away because she's
too young and inexperienced. Mortimer, you shall
stay in here with Penelope.

MORTIMER. Who will help you should the baby's
breathing continue regular?

CAROLINE. I'll call you if I need you, but I wouldn't
allow anybody to do anything at such a time as this.

MORTIMER. Look, you get into bed now. Penelope's
fine out there. I don't want to hear another word.
Should the doctor come, I'll let him in. (MORTIMER
*puts his wife into bed. He blows out the candle. He
lies down on his bed. Pause.* PENELOPE *coughs.*)

CAROLINE. (*Jumping.*) Why!? Why don't that doctor come?! (MORTIMER *lights candles again.*) Mortimer, this room is too warm. Turn off the register—
quick! (MORTIMER *gets out of bed and kneels beside
the bed to adjust the register.*)

CAROLINE. Mortimer.

MORTIMER. Yes, Dearest, Love?

CAROLINE. The medicine, the medicine the doctor
gave us last time when she had a sore throat. It's still
in the drawer there. (MORTIMER *goes over on his knees
to a night table between the beds and takes out a jar
of medicine and a spoon.*) This is foreordained. Mortimer. We have not been living as we ought to; time
and time again I have told you so. See the result. Our
children will never get well. Be thankful if you can
forgive yourself; I never can forgive myself.

MORTIMER. (*Getting up off his knees with the medicine.*) I do not, Dear, live an abandoned life.

CAROLINE. Mortimer!

MORTIMER. Well, God, does *this* seem like an abandoned life? God!

CAROLINE. Do you want to bring the judgment upon baby too?

MORTIMER. Here. (*He hands the medicine to his wife.*)

CAROLINE. (*Rising.*) Every moment is precious now. But . . .

MORTIMER. What now?

CAROLINE. What's the use of medicine when the disease is incurable?

MORTIMER. Where there's life, there's . . .

CAROLINE. Hope? Mortimer, you know no more what you're talking about than the child unborn. As I live, the directions say give one teaspoonful once an hour! Once an hour! As if we had a whole year before us to save this child. Mortimer, please hurry. (*She hands him the medicine and escorts him over to* PENELOPE.) Give the poor perishing thing a tablespoon and be quick.

MORTIMER. My Dear, a tablespoon might—

CAROLINE. Don't drive me frantic! (*She pulls the medicine out of his hand and wakes* PENELOPE. *Then she gives it to her.*) There. There. My precious, my own. It's bitter, but it's good for Nelly—good for mother's precious. It will make you well. There, there, lie back. Go to sleep and pretty soon—oh, I know she can't live till morning. (*She pushes* MORTIMER *back into their room.*) Mortimer, a tablespoon every half hour.

MORTIMER. Yes, Dear.

CAROLINE. Oh, the child needs Belladonna, too. I know she does—and aconite. Get them, Mortimer. Now do let me have my own way. You never let me have my own way. And you know nothing about these things.

MORTIMER. Any fool can see I don't. But let's just try to get some rest and let that medicine take effect. You must rest. If something happened to you, Dearest, who's going to care for all the sick ones here?

CAROLINE. You're right. A few hours sleep just to keep strength. (*She checks the infant. Then they get back into bed. He blows out the light again. Pause.*) Darling.

MORTIMER. Huh?

CAROLINE. That register turned on?

MORTIMER. No.

CAROLINE. I thought so. Turn it on at once. This room is so cold. (MORTIMER *gets out of bed, kneels down again at the register. After he turns it on, he gets back into bed.*) Mortimer.

MORTIMER. Here.

CAROLINE. Dearie, would you mind moving the crib to your side of the bed? It is nearer the register.

MORTIMER. (*He gets out of bed again and stubs his toe on the crib.*) YOU SON OF A—

CAROLINE. Mortimer! The baby! (*Pause. Then* MORTIMER *drags the crib or cradle over to his side and again jumps into bed. Pause.*) Mortimer, Mortimer, if we only had some goose grease to rub on Penelope's throat.

MORTIMER. She doesn't need goose grease. (*Long pause.* PENELOPE *coughs.* MORTIMER *climbs out of bed and exits down the hallway. An animal scream is heard.*)

CAROLINE. Mortimer!

MORTIMER. (*Off.*) I stepped on the cat! (*A crash is heard.*)

CAROLINE. You always bump into that sewing machine. You're going to wake the child. (*Off stage we see a light.*) Why're you lighting the gas?

MORTIMER. (*Off.*) I want to see how much I hurt myself, Caroline.

CAROLINE. Oh. Well look at the sewing machine too. No doubt it's ruined.

MORTIMER. If it's not, it's not my fault: I hit it hard as I could. (*The light goes off.*)

CAROLINE. Now, Mortimer, there's no need for any further remarks. It's a pity. If you can't do the few little things I ask of you at such an awful time as this when our child is—

MORTIMER. (*Entering with a can.*) Here's the goose grease.

CAROLINE. Rub it on the child's chest, please. (*He goes into the sleeping PENELOPE and rubs goose grease on her neck and chest. He gets back into bed.*) Mortimer, don't catch cold yourself now. (MORTIMER *mumbles to himself as he puts the can of goose grease down and crosses back to his own bed.*) Mortimer.

MORTIMER. What?

CAROLINE. I think it's time for her medicine again.

MORTIMER. It is not time. Anyway I have goose grease all over my hands. I'm afraid the medicine, the spoon, and child are just gonna slip out of the room.

CAROLINE. Don't get tart with me. I'll do it myself. Go ahead. Get into your warm bed and enjoy yourself. (*She gets out of bed and crosses into PENELOPE with the medicine.*)

MORTIMER. It isn't a half hour yet.

CAROLINE. (*She puts the medicine down.*) Mortimer, bring me an extra blanket for her. (MORTIMER *gets out of bed, lights the candle, and takes a blanket from the foot of his bed. He crosses again into PENELOPE. She places the blanket over PENELOPE.*) It's all over.

MORTIMER. Huh?

CAROLINE. It's all over. The child's perspiring.

MORTIMER. It's the six blankets and the inch thick layer of goose grease.

CAROLINE. Oh, idiot, it's not that. Please go to bed. You're in my way. (MORTIMER *crosses back to his bed; puts the candle out. She sings* PENELOPE *a lullaby even though* PENELOPE *is asleep.* MORTIMER *tosses and turns.*) Can't you sleep, Mortimer?

MORTIMER. I really don't think I'm here for that, am I?

(*Pounding heard off.*)

CAROLINE. The doctor! (*She runs for her robe and also combs her hair.* MORTIMER *lights the candle. He runs off and returns with the half-dressed doctor.*) Doctor! Thank God. We're all dying here. In here. As you can see, membranous croup.

DOCTOR. (*He wakes* PENELOPE *and examines her throat.*) Whoa, here. Now whoa.

CAROLINE. What did he say?

MORTIMER. Whoa here. Now whoa.

DOCTOR. This child hasn't got membranous croup.

CAROLINE. She has to have it.

DOCTOR. She's been chewing on a bit of pine shingle or something of the kind. She's got some little slivers in her throat. They won't do her no hurt.

MORTIMER. Well, I can believe it. Did you know that the turpentine that's in there is very good for certain diseases? Ask my wife.

(*She leaves the room in a huff.*)

DOCTOR. What's the matter with her?

MORTIMER. She's not well. She became a wife and then was stricken with motherhood, and most serious of all, she is a woman and there is no known cure for any of it, Doctor.

(PENELOPE *coughs.*)

BLACKOUT

COSTUME PLOT

1 female nightgown

1 night robe

1 male nightgown and night cap

1 turn-of-the-century nurse's or governess' costume

1 turn-of-the-century child's dress for Penelope

1 night gown for Penelope

PROPERTY PLOT

several candles on tables

1 piece of wood

papers and charcoal for Penelope to draw

1 jar medicine

1 spoon

1 tin can for goose grease

several extra blankets for the bottom of the beds

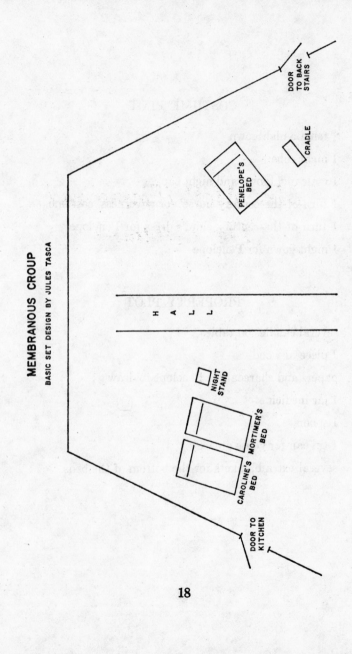

MEMBRANOUS CROUP

BASIC SET DESIGN BY JULES TASCA

DOOR TO BACK STAIRS

CRADLE

PENELOPE'S BED

HALL

NIGHT STAND

CAROLINE'S BED

MORTIMER'S BED

DOOR TO KITCHEN

18

Mrs. McWilliams and The Lightning

CHARACTERS

CAROLINE MCWILLIAMS—A woman sometimes border-
ing on the neurotic because of an intense fear of
lightning. She can be almost any age.

MORTIMER MCWILLIAMS—Caroline's husband. He is a
man who wants to please his wife although she
sometimes makes it impossible. Her neurosis over
lightning storms is eventually transmitted to her
husband.

DESCRIPTION

MRS. McWILLIAMS AND THE LIGHTNING—
1 male, 1 female. 1 male bit part. Classic Mark Twain.
At the opening Mrs. McWilliams is hiding in the closet
frightened of the lightning storm that seems to be
raging outside. Her husband who at first is not afraid
of lightning, becomes just as panicked as his wife and
she sends him through the funniest paces to avoid
being struck: standing on a chair in his nightshirt
wearing a fire hat and spurs while ringing a dinner
bell. The *fole a deux* is broken up only when a neigh-
bor sticks his head in the window at the end to inform
them that there is no lightning storm. What they heard
was cannon fire in celebration of Garfield's nomination for President.

Mrs. McWilliams and The Lightning

(*The stage is dark. A flash of lightning is seen. A clap of thunder immediately follows.*)

WOMAN'S VOICE. (*In the dark.*) Mortimer. Mortimer.

MORTIMER. (*Lights a few candles and we can see we are in a bedroom with a window up Center and a small fireplace Left.*) Caroline? Is that you? Where are you?

CAROLINE. (*Off.*) In the hall closet! You ought to be ashamed to sleep in this storm.

MORTIMER. How can one be ashamed to sleep? It's unreasonable. A man can't be ashamed when he's asleep.

CAROLINE. You never try, Mortimer. You know very well you never try.

(CAROLINE *starts crying.* MORTIMER *gets up, lights other candles and goes off into the wings. He comes back escorting a crying* CAROLINE.)

MORTIMER. I'm sorry, Dear— I'm truly sorry. I never meant to act so. (MORTIMER *sits on the bed.*)

CAROLINE. Mortimer!

MORTIMER. What?

CAROLINE. You're not getting back into bed.

MORTIMER. Of course.

CAROLINE. Get up instantly. I should think you would take some little care of your life for my sake and the sake of your children.

MORTIMER. But, my Love . . .

CAROLINE. Don't, Mortimer, you know there is no place so dangerous as bed in a thunderstorm. You lie there deliberately to throw away your life.

MORTIMER. Confound it, Caroline, I'm . . .

(Another larger glare of lightning and sound of thunder through the curtained window up stage.)

CAROLINE. (*To* MORTIMER *who has jumped out of bed.*) There! See. See the result. Oh, Mortimer, how can you be so profligate as to swear at a time like this?

MORTIMER. I *didn't* swear. And that wasn't a result of it anyway. It would have come just the same if I hadn't said a word. You know very well, Caroline, when the atmosphere is charged with electricity . . .

CAROLINE. Argue it and argue it all you want. Not a lightning rod on the whole place. Your wife at the absolute mercy of providence. Maybe you'd better put the candle out.

MORTIMER. Why?

CAROLINE. It may attract lightning. Are you determined to sacrifice us all? (*More lightning and thunder on top of each other.*) See what you've done?

MORTIMER. No, I don't see what I've done. A candle don't attract lightning— I'll go odds on that. If that last blast was leveled at my candle, it was blessed poor marksmanship.

CAROLINE. For shame, Mortimer. Here we are in the very presence of death and you use language that . . . Mortimer.

MORTIMER. Well?

CAROLINE. Did you say your prayers tonight?

MORTIMER. I meant to. I got busy and . . . (*Another bolt and blast.*)

CAROLINE. We are lost beyond all help! Oh! How could you neglect prayers at a time like this?

MORTIMER. It wasn't a time like this. There wasn't a cloud in the sky. How'd I know there was going to be all this rumpus over a little slip up like this. And I don't think it's just fair for you to make so much out of it anyway. Happens so seldom. I haven't missed before since I brought in that earthquake four years ago.

CAROLINE. How well I remember. And have you forgotten the yellow fever?

MORTIMER. My dear, you always throw the yellow fever up to me and it's unreasonable. You can't even send a telegram as far as Memphis without relays, so how is a little devotional slip of mine gonna carry so far? I stood the earthquake because it was here in the neighborhood, but I'll be hanged if they're gonna pin yellow fever on . . . (*Another huge beroom, boom, boom, bang.*)

CAROLINE. Oh, Dear—Dear—Dear! We won't see the light of another day. When we're gone, Mortimer, remember it was your dreadful language— Mortimer.

MORTIMER. What now?

CAROLINE. Your voice sounds as if— Mortimer, are you standing in front of that open fireplace?

MORTIMER. Yes.

CAROLINE. Get away from it! You know there's no better conductor for lightning than an open chimney. (*He crosses to the window.*) Have you lost your mind?! The very children in arms know it is fatal to stand near a window in a thunderstorm.

MORTIMER. (*Crossing to her.*) Sorry.

CAROLINE. What's that you're rustling?

MORTIMER. I'm putting my pants on.

CAROLINE. Quick, throw them away! All authorities

agree that wool attracts lightning!! (MORTIMER *flings his pants on the bed as if they were red hot in his hands; then he begins to hum in frustration, as he crosses off stage.*) Oh, don't sing!

MORTIMER. (*Off.*) Why not?

CAROLINE. Mortimer, if I told you once, I've told you a hundred times that singing causes vibrations in the atmosphere which interrupts the flow of the electric field— (*The sound of a door opening off.*) Why are you opening that door?

MORTIMER. (*Off.*) Goodness, gracious, woman, is there any harm in that?

CAROLINE. Harm. Oh, no. Just death, that's all. Everyone knows that to create a draft invites lightning. (MORTIMER *shuts the door.*) Shut it tight! (*Sound of water running.*) Lunatic! What are you doing?!

MORTIMER. (*Off.*) Washing my hands.

CAROLINE. You have parted with the remnant of your mind. If lightning strikes anything, it strikes water fifty times. Turn it off! (*Sound of a thump from off stage.*) What was that?

MORTIMER. (*Off.*) I knocked the picture off the wall.

CAROLINE. You are that close to the wall? I never heard of such imprudence. There is no better conductor for lightning than a wall! Come away! Mortimer, did you order a feather bed as I asked you to?

MORTIMER. (*Re-entering left.*) No, I forgot.

CAROLINE. You forgot. Now it may cost you your life. If I had a feather bed now and could lie on it, we'd be perfectly safe.

(*Cat meows.*)

MORTIMER. (*As* CAROLINE *jumps.*) It's only the cat.

CAROLINE. (*Pushing him out of the room.*) Catch her

and shut her up in the bathroom. Cats are full of electricity. Oh, my hair will turn white with this night of peril! (CAROLINE *takes a book from the night table.* MORTIMER *steps on the cat and it screams.*)

MORTIMER. Come here, you little . . . Damn. Damn. Damn. (*More bolts of lightning and thunder.* CAROLINE *screams.* MORTIMER *runs back on stage to her.*) It's all right. It's all right.

CAROLINE. Oh, Mortimer! Look, this book says the safest thing is to stand on a chair in the middle of the room. And the legs of the chair must be insulated with non-conductors. That is, you must sit the legs of the chairs in glass tumblers. (*Another lightning thunder crash.*) Hurry, Mortimer, before we're struck.

MORTIMER. (*He sets a chair in 4 tumblers quickly. He's becoming concerned himself.*) Okay, what does it say now?

CAROLINE. It says, "Wahrend eines Gewitters entferne man metalle, wie 2. B., Ring, uhren, schlussel, etc., von sich und halte sich auch nicht an solchein stellen auf, wo uiele metalle bei einander liegen . . .

MORTIMER. That German book your grandfather left. That's what we're going by?

CAROLINE. I think it means you must keep metal about you, Mortimer.

MORTIMER. I don't remember much German. Maybe it . . .

CAROLINE. No, that's what it means. Put on your fireman's helmet, Mortimer. That's metal. Then I'll hold on to you. (MORTIMER *gets the helmet from under the bed and puts it on.*) Your middle ought to be protected. Put Grandpa's old saber on. (MORTIMER *complies. He's fully involved in* CAROLINE's *plan now.*) Your feet! Put on your spurs. (MORTIMER *takes his spurs and puts them on.*) Now it says, 'Das Gewitter lauten ist sehr gefahrlich, weil die glocke seibst, sowie der durch das Launten veranl asste Luftzug und die Hohe des thumesden Blitz Anziehen Kennten.' Does. that mean it is dangerous not to ring church bells during thunderstorms?

MORTIMER. Yes, it seems to mean that. I think it means that on account of the height of the church tower and the absence of *Luftzug* it would be very dangerous not to ring bells in a storm.

CAROLINE. Run. Get the large dinner bell.

MORTIMER. But . . .

CAROLINE. Mortimer, we're almost safe! (MORTIMER *runs off left.* CAROLINE *fixes the chair and tumblers.* MORTIMER *runs back in with a large dinner bell.*) Up here! We're going to be saved!

(MORTIMER *gets up on the chair and begins to ring the bell.* CAROLINE *climbs up and puts her arms around him. After he rings the bell for several beats the window Center is pulled open from the outside and a lantern is shone in on them.*)

MAN. What's the matter here?

MORTIMER. Nothing friends. Only a little discomfort because of the thunderstorm. I'm warding off lightning.

MAN. Lightning? Thunderstorm? Mr. McWilliams, you lost your mind? It's a beautiful starlit night. There's no storm.

MORTIMER. I don't get it. We saw the glow, the flashes, heard the thunder.

(*Man starts laughing.*)

CAROLINE. What is it?

MAN. Pity you didn't open your blinds and look

over to the top of the hill. What you heard was a cannon. What you saw was the flash. You see, the telegraph brought the news just before midnight: Garfield's nominated for President. (*He continues laughing.* MR. *and* MRS. *look at each other. Then a clap of* "*thunder*" *follows a flash.*)

BLACKOUT

COSTUME PLOT

Male—nightgown for Mortimer

Female—nightgown for Caroline

PROPERTY PLOT

several candles and holders

1 pair of pants at the bottom of Mortimer's bed
an old leather bound book for the night table drawer

4 glass tumblers

1 fire helmet

1 sabre with belt

1 pair spurs

1 dinner bell

1 lantern

MRS. MC WILLIAMS AND THE LIGHTNING

SET DESIGN BY JULES TASCA

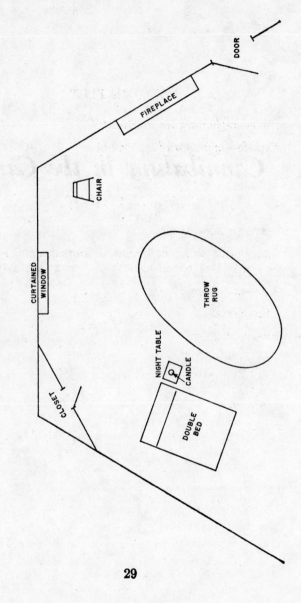

Cannibalism in the Cars

CHARACTERS

Eight Congressmen, easily recognized types. One is an old man. One is a chauvinistic Democrat. One a Republican who puts him down.

Two train porters or conductors.

One Engineer.

DESCRIPTION

CANNIBALISM IN THE CARS—11 males—is adapted from one of Mark Twain's most amusing short stories. It deals with 8 Congressmen riding a train to Washington, who become trapped for over two months in an inpenetrable snow drift. They do the only thing possible when they run out of food. They form a committee to decide who amongst them should be eaten first. They make nominations for breakfast as though they were in the Halls of Congress, and vote for the most succulent member as if it were a highway construction bill until the group is down to just two: two rivals, a Democrat and a Republican who must decide which one will be the next meal.

Cannibalism in the Cars

(This piece is simply done by arranging folding chairs on stage to represent a turn-of-the-century passenger train. As the curtain rises 8 Congressmen dressed in turn-of-the-century attire eat, smoke and drink as they await the resumption of their train ride to Washington.)

GASTON. When are they going to get this train moving again?

WILLIAMS. We're never goin' to make it for the openin' of Congress.

GASTON. They should have a special train for us Congressmen instead of just a private car.

SAWYER. Maybe they shouldn't have all us Congressmen on one train at the same time. You know, if something happened, a derailment or something, a whole section of Congress could be completely wiped out.

ADAMS. What would the country do?

SLOATE. Some people would say why does God see fit to smile on us like this.

ADAMS. I'm not kidding, Mr. Sloate.

LANGDON. Nothing's going to happen. They merely stopped for a snow drift, Mr. Adams. They're clearing the tracks now. Just sit down and finish your lunch.

CONDUCTOR. *(Coming in through the back of the rows of chairs.)* Gentlemen.

ALL. Yes.

CONDUCTOR. We are . . .

LANGDON. Yes, man, what is it?

CONDUCTOR. We are snowbound.

BASCOM. Oh, no. We're 70 miles from the nearest town either way.

ADAMS. You want us to help dig it out?

SLOATE. A member of Congress, Mr. Adams, should not be seen with a shovel—makes people think he's hiding something.

ADAMS. This is not funny, Mr. Sloate. Seventy miles from anywhere. Stuck in a snow drift!

LANGDON. Stop shouting. They'll send another train in with food and . . .

VAN NOSTRAD. (*Old and grey.*) Will they, Conductor?

CONDUCTOR. (*Helping* VAN NOSTRAD *to sit down.*) Being members of Congress in this car, I'm gonna give it to you straight: We're hemmed in here, Gentlemen. Avalanches have piled up ahead and behind us. The bearings on the locomotive are burned out trying to plow through the drift. I don't know how long we'll be here. There's plenty of fuel, but no food. That's the picture.

VAN NOSTRAD. Oh, God. Oh, Heaven.

BASCOM. We'll walk it. We'll walk the 70 miles.

ADAMS. I paid to ride.

SLOATE. Your constituency paid for you to ride.

ADAMS. Is that a metaphor, sir?

LANGDON. Nobody's going to walk. You'd freeze to death walking out there.

(*They all look out the window on one side and observe that* LANGDON *is right. It is bad. They back down into their seats.*)

BASCOM. Nothing but white walls.

CONDUCTOR. He's right.

LANGDON. What do you suggest, Conductor?

CONDUCTOR. (*At the back of the row ready to leave.*) Okay, you say no food; you say you're trapped, no where to go, freezing weather outside. I say keep your spirits up. (*He exits.*)

ADAMS. Keep our spirits up?

SLOATE. He's a conductor. What'd you want, the 23rd Psalm?

ADAMS. As august members of the Congress of the United States, I say that we pass the time in this here compartment by doing what we're paid for, discussing and acting on the nation's business.

(*They all look at* ADAMS *for a beat.*)

SLOATE. Did you hear the one about the barmaid with one buttock?

(*They all rush around* SLOATE *who begins to tell the story as the lights fade. When the lights come up again, it is several days later. The Congressmen are all snoring in their seats. Sound of wind howling outside. Old* VAN NOSTRAD *wakes up, wakes up out of a dream.*)

VAN NOSTRAD. More Yorkshire pudding, Waiter! More Yorkshire pudding, Waiter! More . . .

(*They all wake up with a start.*)

ADAMS. What was that?

BASCOM. Van Nostrad. Dreaming.

VAN NOSTRAD. I was in Washington. The President had invited us for supper. The waiter. He was serving. I . . . I . . .

ADAMS. Yorkshire pudding. How was it? Last night you were in an oyster eating contest and Bascom was yelling in his sleep about a cow's teat.

SAWYER. That's nothing. Me. I ate the other buttock.

LANGDON. Mr. Sawyer!

SAWYER. It's true—with tabasco sauce.

SLOATE. Seven days without food. Everybody's been talking in his sleep about food except Mr. Adams. He gave a political speech.

ADAMS. I do not, Sir, talk in my sleep.

SLOATE. Don't be angry, I think you were re-elected.

LANGDON. Stop it, you two. You fight every day in Washington. We're starving to death and you still can't stop fighting.

GASTON. We're going to get out of this. I know we are. Aren't we? (*Silence.*) Aren't we? (*Silence.*) Well?

SAWYER. Sure. Sure we are.

GASTON. I don't know about you, but I can't go on anymore without something to eat. My wallet is lamb skin. I tried to eat it last night.

CONDUCTOR. (*Coming in.*) Gentlemen, I have some further bad news for you.

SLOATE. Don't tell me. Mr. Adams has a twin brother on board.

LANGDON. Shhhh! Go on, man.

CONDUCTOR. We've sealed off. That is, we've locked the first two cars.

SAWYER. Whatever for?

CONDUCTOR. Gentlemen, they have become uncontrollable and . . .

LANGDON. Yes.

CONDUCTOR. There has been an incident of cannibalism. (*Pause. Some of the Congressmen begin to pray.*)

ADAMS. Cannibalism!?

SAWYER. I cant' . . . God . . .

CONDUCTOR. They're up there now having breakfast.

LANGDON. Good Lord!

CONDUCTOR. Her name was Rosemary McNulty. (*He begins to leave.*) Keep your wits about you. Just keep your wits about you. (*He leaves. Silence.*)

ADAMS. We don't have to worry. I am almost certain that it is a Federal offense to eat a Congressman, isn't it?

VAN NOSTRAD. We all sit in disgust, but they're having breakfast in car 1.

ADAMS. Rosemary McNulty. I wonder if she was a Democrat.

GASTON. I have a feeling this is what it's going to come to. I'm sick. I'm sick. I'm sick. To think that's what it's come to.

VAN NOSTRAD. Let's face it, Gentlemen, it has come to that. It'll be months before a thaw sets in. I know these parts. It has come to *that*.

GASTON. (*To* SAWYER.) Whatever happens, Mr. Sawyer—we've backed each other on so many votes. I promise I'll never dine on you.

SAWYER. Thank you. I'm glad to know I still have your support on this. You'll get my vote on the Bull Frog dam project as soon as we get back to . . .

VAN NOSTRAD. If we ever do get back to . . . I don't know. I've seen it before on a wagon train to the West. It has come to cannibalism, Gentlemen.

(*Pause. Silence. They look at each other.* GASTON *removes* SAWYER'S *arm from his own back.*)

SLOATE. I nominate Congressman Harold B. Adams.

ADAMS. For what!!

CONDUCTOR. (*Sticking his head in.*) Anybody in here got a stomach powder?

SAWYER. No.

CONDUCTOR. Somebody in 1 overate. (*He exits.*)

BASCOM. Overate?

LANGDON. Look, if we're going to do this, how do we . . .

VAN NOSTRAD. Same way we do things in Washington. We form a committee and follow the rules.

BASCOM. Wait a minute. My stomach is turning inside out too, but we can't do this just to stay alive. There has to be an alternative to cannibalism.

VAN NOSTRAD. What?

BASCOM. I don't know. Maybe . . . I don't know— Maybe there's something left of Rosemary McNulty that cars 1 and 2 would sell us and . . . (*Silence. He realizes what he's said.*)

ADAMS. Who's going to chair this committee?

LANGDON. Mr. Van Nostrad has seniority.

ADAMS. That's for sure.

VAN NOSTRAD. (*Very business like.*) Meeting come to order. What we have to do— I'm trying to be delicate now—is make a selection.

SLOATE. (*Standing on a box.*) Mr. Chairman—this committee being properly devised, I move to again nominate Mr. Harold B. Adams. I respect him and esteem him as much as any Republican can esteem a Democrat, but it is our duty here to trim waste from the project. He being the plumpest and having the most nutrient as it were, I . . .

ADAMS. I object!!

(MR. SLOATE *steps down.*)

VAN NOSTRAD. Quiet. Any more nominations for breakfast?

BASCOM. Gentlemen, I move to make another nomination not because of personal preference, but from the standpoint of common sense. The hard going of frontier life has rendered Mr. Adams tough. Is this a time to cavil over trifles—yes. We are talking about consumption here, about breakfast. Since Mr. Sawyer and Mr. Gaston are friends and come and go as a pair, I nominate both Mr. Sawyer and Mr. Gaston.

(SAWYER *and* GASTON *grab each other.*)

VAN NOSTRAD. Pass the ballots out and mark your preference.

ADAMS. (*Handing out ballots.*) Thanks, Mr. Bascom. I'll remember this on your Route 36 Highway Bill.

BLACKOUT

(*When the lights come back up, bones are strewn around the car, several skulls with hats. The Conductor's hat is on one of the skulls. These props could be in the Congressmen's luggage and pockets and be placed about as they exit during the blackout.*

ADAMS *and* SLOATE *are the only two survivors. They are smoking cigars; they look complacent and stuffed.* ADAMS *belches.*)

ADAMS. The Conductor was good, but, quite frankly, Mr. Langdon was tough.

SLOATE. The Conductor walked in while we were preparing Van Nostrad and helped himself. It was only fair that we swore him in as an honorary member of Congress.

ADAMS. Hmmm.

SLOATE. (*Holding up a letter.*) Oh, I wrote Mr. Sawyer's wife so if they find the car . . .

ADAMS. Mr. Sawyer was good—a little rare, but good.

SLOATE. I liked Mr. Williams. I would've liked Mr. Williams a little less done.

ADAMS. They voted the quiet Mr. Williams in by acclamation. They knew a calf when they saw one.

SLOATE. I felt Sawyer was crunchier. Sawyer spoke several languages, educated, handsome, and crunchy. In fact, I'd say that Congressman Sawyer was one of the finest men I ever sat down to.

(*In the distance the sound of a train coming in.*)

ADAMS. All that voting. All that lobbying. All the deals and what did it get us?

SLOATE. This. An empty train. Just you and me.

ADAMS. I'm thinking ahead to weekend dinner. How do we vote on this one?

SLOATE. Would you consider voting against yourself— No. I'm not thinking.

ADAMS. What's that?

(*Sound of a train pulling up.* SLOATE *and* ADAMS *jump up and shout out the window.*)

SLOATE. Hey, look!

ADAMS. They found us!!

(*Another Conductor and the train's engineer come in through the back row of the train. They are stunned at the piles of bones.*)

SLOATE. We're saved!

CONDUCTOR. The Congressional car!

ADAMS. After 2½ months I could kiss both of you! I'm Congressman Adams! This is Congressman Sloate! But I'm the Democrat. (*The engineer and the Conductor are too dumbfounded to say anything.*) You're standing on Congressman Bascom.

ENGINEER. (*Finally.*) We got food for youse on the train, Sir.

SLOATE. Me? I couldn't eat a thing.

ADAMS. (*Belches.*) Me either. Langdon went down the wrong pipe.

CONDUCTOR. (*Picking up a skull.*) Congressman Philip E. Langdon? I voted for him. He was supposed to be in Washington working with the railroad lobby.

ADAMS. He had a wooden leg which was a clear loss but otherwise . . .

SLOATE. He was quite good, but if you have some after dinner mints, thanks.

ADAMS. (*Picking up two skulls.*) Oh, it's all done legal. I got the minutes of the meeting. (*Addressing the skulls.*) Mr. Van Nostrad, do you hear? We're saved! Sawyer, we made it! Hey, everybody, we made it! (*To the Engineer and Conductor.*) Grab our suitcases, boys.

(MR. SLOATE *and* MR. ADAMS *put on their hats and walk out the back of the rows of chairs.* CONDUCTOR *picks up two skulls.*)

CONDUCTOR. Proof positive. This is the greatest political system in the world! The great American system works and we owe it to one thing.

ENGINEER. What's that?

CONDUCTOR. (*Holding up* LANGDON's *skull.*) The way our Congressmen can cooperate with one another.

BLACKOUT

COSTUME PLOT

8 turn-of-the-century hats

8 turn-of-the-century suits

2 porters' outfits.

1 engineer's overalls

1 engineer's red bandana

1 engineer's hat

PROPERTY PLOT

several pieces of paper for ballots

nuts and fruit for opening

bones for closing

skulls with hats for closing

Support Your Local Police

CHARACTERS

MR. SIMONS—A representative of a transport company who is delivering an elephant to the President of the U.S. He is worried because his elephant has been stolen.

INSPECTOR BLUNT—A shrewd unscrupulous chief of police who wants to track down the elephant for his own personal gain.

ALARAC—A functionary of the City of New York's police department. He tries to please the Inspector, his boss.

DESCRIPTION

SUPPORT YOUR LOCAL POLICE—3 males—A free adaptation of Mark Twain's satire about the disappearance of a Siamese elephant. Mr. Simons has lost the elephant and places the case in the hands of a maniacal police chief who is out for nothing but personal gain. Meanwhile, the lost elephant roams New York, squirting water at the Anti-Temperance League, destroying a plumber, breaking up a funeral, breaking up a revival meeting, and stepping on a preacher. At the conclusion, the police chief has the reward and the credit for ridding New York of the elephant and Simons is put in jail for leaving an elephant over 24 hours in a public place.

Support Your Local Police

(*Lights come up on a police headquarters.* INSPECTOR BLUNT *sits at his desk. An assistant, in uniform,* ALARAC, *sits at another desk upon which is a telegraph key. A middle aged well-dressed gentleman,* MR. SIMONS, *runs in excitedly.*)

MR. SIMONS. My name is Simons. I wanted to report a theft. Who do I see?

INSPECTOR. (*As* ALARAC *points without looking.*) I am *the* Inspector Blunt. If there is anything missing, I'll find it.

ALARAC. He finds everything. Found a woman's dog once and she didn't even own a dog.

MR. SIMONS. Thank God I've come to the right place.

INSPECTOR. What is lost?

MR. SIMONS. Stolen.

INSPECTOR. It is your wife, Sir? Give me a pair of her underwear and ten days and I'll . . .

MR. SIMONS. It's an elephant, Inspector.

(*Pause.* ALARAC *turns around for the first time.*)

INSPECTOR. (*Rises.*) Mr. Simons, allow me to think a moment. This will be no ordinary case.

ALARAC. He's so sharp.

INSPECTOR. Every step must be warily taken. Secrecy must be observed. Speak to no one about the matter, not even the reporters who loiter about here. (*He snaps his fingers and* ALARAC *crosses to him with a notebook and pencil.*) What, Simons, are you doing with an elephant? Most people simply marry and play bridge.

MR. SIMONS. My company, World Wide Shipping, is in charge of delivering an elephant as a gift from the King of Siam to the President of the United States.

ALARAC. My God. My God. My God.

INSPECTOR. He's not your God alone, Alarac. Stop being so possessive.

MR. SIMONS. I came with him from Siam by freighter. He was penned up in the lumber yard across the street from your headquarters here. He was to go to Washington by train.

INSPECTOR. Hm. Hm. Gift for the President from the King of Siam. Was there anything for me?

MR. SIMONS. I wasn't aware you knew the King of Siam.

INSPECTOR. I don't. I thought he might've heard of me—no matter. No king is well informed anymore. Name of the elephant?

MR. SIMONS. (*As* ALARAC *writes.*) Hassen Ben ali Ben Selim abdallah Mohammed Moise al hammal Jamsetyeyecbhoy Dhuleys Sulton Ebu Bhadpoor.

INSPECTOR. Very well. Given name?

MR. SIMONS. Jumbo.

INSPECTOR. Place of birth?

MR. SIMONS. Siam.

INSPECTOR. Parents living?

MR. SIMONS. Dead.

INSPECTOR. Had they any other issue besides this one?

MR. SIMONS. No, he was an only child.

INSPECTOR. Hmm. Family planning is world wide. Please describe this elephant. Leave out nothing.

MR. SIMONS. Well . . . height, 19 feet. Length from forehead to tail, 26 feet. Trunk, 16 feet. Tail, 6 feet. Tusks, 9½ feet. Footprints resemble the mark left when one upends a barrel in the snow. Color, white. Let's see . . . has a hole in each ear the size of a plate for earrings. Oh, yes, a small scar on left armpit from having a boil removed. When stolen, he was wearing a castle containing seats for 15 persons and a gold cloth saddle blanket the size of a carpet.

INSPECTOR. (*To* ALARAC.) Have 50,000 copies of this printed at once and mailed to every detective office and pawn brokers shop.

ALARAC. Yes, Sir. (*He exits.*)

MR. SIMONS. Pawn brokers?

INSPECTOR. Thieves in New York pawn anything. Standard procedure. I'll need a photograph.

MR. SIMONS. (*Pulling out his wallet and taking a picture from it.*) Here you are.

INSPECTOR. Hmm. It must do if it's the only one you have. I would have preferred a front view rather than a rear view. Might mislead. Of course, if my men should spot him from the front, they're trained to put 2 and 2 together. (*To* ALARAC *coming back in.*) 50,000 of these pictures to accompany the circulars.

ALARAC. This is a rear view, Sir.

INSPECTOR. I'm not impressed, Alarac. Promotion denied.

ALARAC. Yes, Sir. (*He exits again with the photograph.*)

INSPECTOR. We generally get an inkling of who our thief is by the manner of his work and the size of the game he goes after. This is no pickpocket. This was a professional job. There are cases I've cracked that show we can trace people through personal habits. What does this elephant eat and how much? (*To* ALARAC *who has reentered.*) Alarac, take it all down.

MR. SIMONS. Well, as to what he eats—he will eat anything. He will eat a man; he will eat a Bible—he will eat anything between a man and a Bible.

INSPECTOR. Good—very good, indeed, but too general. Details, Simons. Details. As to men. At one meal —how many men will he eat, if fresh?

MR. SIMONS. Five.

INSPECTOR. What nationalities would he prefer?

MR. SIMONS. He doesn't discriminate. He prefers acquaintances but is not prejudiced against strangers.

INSPECTOR. Very good. Now as to Bibles. How many Bibles would he eat at a meal?

MR. SIMONS. An entire edition.

INSPECTOR. Hardly succinct enough. Do you mean the ordinary octave or the family illustrated?

MR. SIMONS. I think he would be indifferent to illustrations. I think he wouldn't value illustrations above simple letter press.

INSPECTOR. Put it in dollars and cents. At 100 dollars a good leather bound copy, how much would he eat?

MR. SIMONS. $50,000 worth.

INSPECTOR. 500 copies. Now that's more exact. What else would he eat. I want particulars. Particulars.

MR. SIMONS. He'll eat bricks, bottles; he will leave bottles to eat clothing; he will leave clothing to eat cats; he will leave cats to eat oysters; leave oysters to eat ham; leave ham to eat sugar; leave sugar to eat pie; leave pie to eat bran; leave bran to eat oats; leave oats to eat rice— There is nothing on God's earth he wouldn't eat but European butter and he'd eat that if he could taste it.

Inspector. General quantities per meal.

Mr. Simons. Quarter to half a ton.

Inspector. And he drinks.

Mr. Simons. Everything that is fluid: milk, water, molasses, oil, carbolic acid. He will drink anything but European coffee.

Inspector. Very good. As to quantity?

Mr. Simons. (*To* Alarac.) Put down 5 to 15 barrels.

Inspector. Alarac, detail Detectives Jones, Halsey, Bates, and Hacket to shadow the elephant.

Alarac. Got it, Sir.

Inspector. Detail Detectives Moser, Dakin, Murphy, Rogers, Tupper, Higgins, and Bartholemew to shadow the thieves.

Alarac. Yes, Sir.

Mr. Simons. Who are the thieves?

Inspector. Never interrupt a law enforcer in the line of duty, Sir. Alarac, keep reporters away. Place detectives in plain clothes at all railway, ferry, and steamboat depots with orders to search all suspicious persons.

Mr. Simons. For what?

Inspector. There you are again. I did not interfere with your transporting the elephant, Mr. Simons; do not interfere with me apprehending the beast.

Mr. Simons. I'm sorry. I'm in your hands.

Inspector. (*To* Alarac.) Put out orders that all information or clues in this case should be sent to this room by telegraph.

Alarac. Yes, Sir.

Inspector. Dispatch plainclothes men all over the New York area. I am not given to boasting, Mr. Simons, but no one can find this elephant without me. (Alarac *again exits to carry out orders.*) You would do well,

Mr. Simons, to put up a reward. How much will your company spring for?

MR. SIMONS. We're prepared for that. I have with me $25,000.

INSPECTOR. (*Snatching it out of his hand and pocketing it.*) That will do to begin with.

MR. SIMONS. To begin with. Oh, yes. Oh, sure. To begin with. I don't know how to thank you, Sir.

INSPECTOR. Anyway you like, Simons, as long as it's loud and often.

(*Black out. Lights come up again almost immediately.
ALARAC is at the telegraph key. INSPECTOR BLUNT
is counting money at his desk. MR. SIMONS rushes
in with several newspapers. BLUNT quickly puts
the money away.*)

MR. SIMONS. Look at these papers. Each one has a different story.

INSPECTOR. You don't think we gave out only one story, Mr. Simons. Have you no interest in nuance?

MR. SIMONS. I will not pretend to know all the workings of the police department . . .

INSPECTOR. Too bad. We could've used you in our uptown office.

MR. SIMONS. . . . but this. (*Reads from a newspaper.*) "The Chief Inspector, Marcus Blunt, who knew the crooks were Brick Duffy and Reds McFadden ten days before the robbery of the elephant, said he was aware of the elephant caper plans."

INSPECTOR. Duffy and McFadden, boldest scoundrels in the profession.

ALARAC. They stole the stove out of the detective headquarters last winter. Every detective was at the doctors with frozen fingers, ears, and other members.

INSPECTOR. Enough bragging, Alarac.

MR. SIMONS. But if you knew . . .

INSPECTOR. It is not our province to prevent crime but to punish it. We cannot punish it until it is committed.

MR. SIMONS. And I thought you wanted no reporters.

INSPECTOR. We must keep in with them, Simons. Fame, reputation, constant public mention. These are the detective's bread and butter. He must publish fact else he'll seem to have none. Show the public you are doing something—anything—or they'll think you're doing nothing. If you feel I'm inconsistent, think how McFadden and Duffy are being thrown.

MR. SIMONS. The paper also said the $25,000 reward was for the detective who found the elephant. I thought it ought to be offered to anybody who caught it.

INSPECTOR. (*Laughs.*) It is the detectives who will find the elephant, Simons. We are trained to be sagacious. You think just anyone can be sagacious? It's a common error. I forgive you.

(*Telegraph key starts clicking away.* ALARAC *records the message as* BLUNT *and* SIMONS *gather around the telegraph key.*)

ALARAC. Darly reporting in, Sir, from Flower Station. Have got a clue—found succession of deep tracks across a farm near here—followed two miles east without results—think elephant went west—Brooks has been shadowing him in that direction, Darly.

INSPECTOR. Darly, one of our best men. We must find some money somewhere and have his glasses fixed.

Simons. He can't see?

Inspector. Only when looking directly into the sun.

(*Telegraph starts again.*)

Alarac. Baker, Sir. Just arrived. Glass factory broken into here in New Jersey—800 bottles taken—only water in large quantities 5 miles distant—shall strike for there—elephant will be thirsty—bottles were empty, Baker.

Inspector. I told you the creatures appetite would be good clues.

(*Telegraph again.*)

Alarac. Taylor on Long Island. A hay stack here disappeared during the night—probably eaten—am off, Taylor.

Inspector. He's got some quick moves, this animal.

Mr. Simons. The elephant?

Inspector. No, Taylor. I hope his wife never catches him.

(*Telegraph.*)

Alarac. Flower Station again, Sir. Shadowed track three miles—large, deep and ragged— Have farmer who says they are not elephant tracks— Says they are holes where he dug up saplings for shade tree, Brooks.

Inspector. Ahh! A confederate of thieves. Wire back to Brooks. Arrest farmer and force him to name pals— Continue to follow tracks to Canada if necessary, Blunt.

(*Telegraph clicks in another message as* SIMONS *takes a quick drink of liquor from* ALARAC'S *desk.*)

ALARAC. Murph, Sir. At Coney Point. Gas office broken into during night— Three months' unpaid gas bills taken— Am on his trail, Love, Murph.

INSPECTOR. Love? Tell Detective Murphy to stop using our time for personal messages. Gas bills. Would he eat gas bills?

MR. SIMONS. Oh, I don't know at this point. Through ignorance, maybe, but they cannot support life and . . .

(*The telegraph key chatters on.*)

ALARAC. Haws, Sir. Elephant passed Lubac Village. Some say he went North— Some say South— Some say West— Some say East— Am following him, Haws.

MR. SIMONS. I'm getting a little tired, Sir. Now how in blazes does he know which direction to go in?!

INSPECTOR. The layman's mind! Have you not heard of the needleless compass, Simons?

ALARAC. Sage Corners reporting.

MR. SIMONS. (*To the audience.*) Needleless compass?

ALARAC Elephant passed through here at 8:15— All escaped from town but a policeman— Elephant apparently did not strike at policeman, but at lamppost— Got both— I have secured a portion of the policeman as clue— Best regards, Strum.

SIMONS. Oh, I feel so bad.

INSPECTOR. Over a lamppost?

ALARAC. Brant, Sir. Village of Glover deserted except for sick and aged— Elephant passed through ¾ of an hour ago— The anti-temperance mass meeting was in session— He put his trunk in at window and washed it out with water from cistern— Some swallowed it— Since dead— Several drowned— People fleeing their homes, Brant.

SIMONS. Those poor innocent people.

INSPECTOR. No one is innocent, Simons, only uncaught. We're closing in on him.

ALARAC. O'Flaterty reporting in, Sir. Just missed elephant— Passed through Hogan's Street before I arrived— Wild fright— Two plumbers going by— Killed one— Other escaped— Regret General, O'Flaterty.

INSPECTOR. He's in the midst of my men. Nothing can save him.

SIMONS. I want you to know that . . . that my company will pay for these funerals.

INSPECTOR. Enough levity, Simons. Another message. Who is it now?

ALARAC. P. T. Barnum.

SIMONS. P. T. Barnum? *The* P. T. Barnum?

ALARAC. I offer rate of $4,000 a year for exclusive privilege of using elephant as traveling advertising medium from now till detectives find him— Want to paste circus posters on him— Answer immediately, P. T. Barnum, New York. New York.

SIMONS. That's absurd.

INSPECTOR. Of course it is. Evidently Mr. Barnum who thinks he is sharp does not know me. Wire back; "offer declined—make it $7,000 or nothing."

MR. SIMONS. But Inspector, this animal belongs to the President.

INSPECTOR. He's got the first lady. The way I see it, that's more than enough.

ALARAC. Barnum's reply, Sir: Done. P. T. Barnum.

MR. SIMONS. I can't believe it! The President's elephant!

INSPECTOR. Relax, Simons. I know my business. Barnum's men'll never find the elephant.

ALARAC. Burke and Muldoon checking in. Bolivia Avenue. Elephant was here— Dispersed a funeral— Diminished mourners by two— Citizens fired cannon balls at the beast— Detective Burke seized the tail and exclaimed: "I claim the region for the President of the United States of . . ."—Got no further— A single blow of the trunk on Burke made him ask for sick leave— Beast turned to me and I would be on sick leave too but remains of funeral intervened again and diverted his attention— Nothing of funeral left— But this is no loss, for there is abundance of material for another, Muldoon.

MR. SIMONS. Oh, God. Why couldn't the King of Siam send the President a parrot?

INSPECTOR. Up the reward, Mr. Simons. It's the only way we can insure continued pressure on the beast. I am never wrong.

MR. SIMONS. Up the reward?

INSPECTOR. I'm never wrong.

MR. SIMONS. $25,000 is a considerable sum, Sir, and . . .

INSPECTOR. I am never wrong.

MR. SIMONS. I don't think . . .

INSPECTOR. I am never, never wrong.

ALARAC. Brent coming in, Sir.

INSPECTOR. Yes.

ALARAC. Elephant here at Baxter Center— Has been plastered with circus bills—

MR. SIMONS. Oh, no!

ALARAC. He broke up a revival, striking down many who were on the point of entering upon a better life— Badly wounded by cannon shots— Proceeded to identify elephant— All marks tallied exactly except one—

We couldn't see the boil scar under arm pit— Detective Brown crept under to look— Detective Brown dead— Elephant off again, Brent. Brown, Sir. Dead. Your son-in-law.

(INSPECTOR BLUNT *looks at* MR. SIMONS. SIMONS *takes out his wallet and empties another pile of bills on* BLUNT'S *desk as the lights fade.*

Again the lights come up almost immediately. BLUNT *is humming and smoking a big cigar.* ALARAC *sits at the desk with the telegraph key. He is asleep. Papers are piled high on his desk.* MR. SIMONS *again rushes in carrying newspapers again.*)

INSPECTOR. Ah, Simons.

MR. SIMONS. What are we going to do? Every paper you buy has tales of fire, pillage, death, destruction. And no elephant. (*Pause.*) How can you sit there so calm? Three days ago your son-in-law was struck down dead.

INSPECTOR. Every time an officer of the law gets under an elephant's arm pit, he knows there are risks. Besides, my daughter remarried this morning.

MR. SIMONS. Already?

INSPECTOR. Mourning too long ruins the spirit. As for me. This is the greatest windfall a detective ever had. Look at these papers. The fame. The fame.

MR. SIMONS. Fame? Fame, sure. Look at the lies. "Inspector Blunt guarantees capture soon." You're famous. Me. I'm responsible to my company. Look at this list of crimes. (*Going through the newspapers.*) "Citizens at polls struck down by scourge of Siam." "Elephant steps on preacher." "Elephant kills lightning insurance salesman." "Elephant sits on entire school board." And on and on and on.

INSPECTOR. If your company can deliver another $25,000 reward, I can guarantee the beast's return.

MR. SIMONS. Another . . . Will we have the elephant today?

INSPECTOR. You look like a man of taste, Mr. Simons. Put up another $25,000 and see.

MR. SIMONS. Not unless you can deliver the elephant back here today.

INSPECTOR. In the words of Barnum, Done.

MR. SIMONS. (*He empties another wallet full of bills on the desk. He sits down.*) I shall wait.

INSPECTOR. (*Pocketing the bills.*) No need to wait. Look out the window here. (*He escorts* MR. SIMONS *to the edge of the stage and* MR. SIMONS *looks down.*)

MR. SIMONS. It's him! It's him! Asleep in the back of the police yard! How!?

INSPECTOR. He wandered in here night before last.

MR. SIMONS. And you told no one?

INSPECTOR. We had to milk it for all it was worth.

MR. SIMONS. What about Duffy and McFadden?

INSPECTOR. Hanged a year ago.

MR. SIMONS. But how did . . .

INSPECTOR. Your pacyderm merely bit off the lock and walked out of the pen. I checked the lock myself the first day.

MR. SIMONS. Then Duffy and McFadden were . . .

INSPECTOR. Publicity.

MR. SIMONS. And what you told the papers . . .

INSPECTOR. Duplicity.

MR. SIMONS. And your behavior is due to . . .

INSPECTOR. Eccentricity.

MR. SIMONS. The poor thing's asleep.

INSPECTOR. Not asleep.

MR. SIMONS. You mean?

INSPECTOR. Yes. The cannon shots wounded Hassen fatally.

MR. SIMONS. Dead? But. But. You cost me $75,000 for . . .

INSPECTOR. I kept my part of the bargain, Sir. Alarac built it up in the papers. How I directed the whole procedure. How I directed the entire group of detectives and how I single-handedly saved the city from Jumbo.

MR. SIMONS. You! You! I'll spill everything I know.

INSPECTOR. Mr. Simons, you have been responsible for a decaying elephant loitering up the property of the City of New York. Leaving an elephant 24 hours in a public place constitutes a felony on the part of the owner or custodian. However, I think I can get you a light sentence if you cooperate. Alarac, arrest him.

MR. SIMONS. (*As* ALARAC *rises and takes his arm.*) I'll sue you!

INSPECTOR. A national hero. I doubt it.

(*Telegraph clicks.* ALARAC *goes to the telegraph key.*)

ALARAC. Darly, Sir. First time I've struck a telegraph office in 3 days— Have followed footprints on horseback— They're getting bigger and fresher— Don't worry, Sir. Inside of another week, I'll have that elephant dead sure, Darly— Somewhere outside Cleveland, Ohio. Shall I wire him the truth, Sir?

INSPECTOR. (*Taking his hat and cane and exiting.*) No. Give him his lead, Alarac. No telling what he'll come up with. Good day, Mr. Simons. See you in court.

(*Lights fade. Music up as* ALARAC *picks up a ring of keys and marches* MR. SIMONS *off to jail.*)

COSTUME PLOT

two turn-of-the-century suits with hats for Mr. Simons
   and Inspector Blunt

one turn-of-the-century police uniform for Alarac

PROPERTY PLOT

1 telegraph key for Alarac's desk

1 notebook and pencil

1 photograph of elephant (not seen by audience)

1 wallet for Mr. Simons

several packs of stage money for Simons' reward

several newspapers

1 bottle of liquor for Alarac's desk

1 glass

1 cigar for Inspector Blunt

1 cane for Inspector Blunt

1 pair of handcuffs for Alarac's belt

1 ring with keys for Alarac's desk

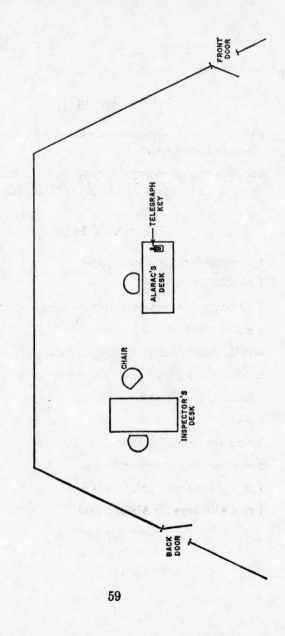

SUPPORT YOUR LOCAL POLICE

BASIC SET DESIGN BY JULES TASCA

FRONT DOOR

TELEGRAPH KEY

ALARAC'S DESK

CHAIR

INSPECTOR'S DESK

BACK DOOR

A Medieval Romance

DESCRIPTION

A MEDIEVAL ROMANCE—Adapted from the sketch by Mark Twain. The Lord of Brandenburgh in order to obtain all the wealth of his brother Ulrich, hides the sex of his daughter from birth, for only a male may inherit the kingdom. A complication arises when Ulrich's daughter, Constance, falls in love with the Lord's daughter, Conrad, who is going around as a handsome Duke. Of course she will have nothing to do with her cousin which angers Constance. When Ulrich's daughter becomes pregnant and is on trial in disgrace for being with child out of wedlock, she accuses Conrad of being the father. Now Conrad, the Lord's daughter, must marry Constance in order to save his own life. The result is a hilarious satire on man's avarice.

A Medieval Romance

*(Light comes up on a Medieval herald. He sends out
a blast on a trumpet and then announces.)*

HERALD. Ladies and Gentlemen. We now take you
back to the Middle Ages, a time when men were men.
As a point of clarification, let me add there were
women in the Middle Ages also. They just didn't brag
about it as much. This is Part I: The Secret Revealed.
Oh God, I can't wait!

*(The lights come up full now. There is a throne on the
stage and several banners surrounding it. The
banner in the center reads "Klugenstien." Seated
on the throne is the old Lord of Klugenstien.
Next to him on a smaller throne sits his wife.
Everyone in the place is dressed in Medieval
costumes. A young knight in armor enters and
kneels.)*

LORD. My daughter!

CONRAD (THE KNIGHT). Speak, Father.

LORD. It is time, my daughter; I must reveal the
mystery to you.

CONRAD. Yes, Father, I've been waiting.

LORD. My brother, Ulrich, the great Duke of Brandenburgh . . .

CONRAD. What has he to do with it?

LORD. Conrad, my father decreed that if no son were
born to Ulrich, I would get all the lands of his king-

don, provided a son were born to me. If no son were born to either Ulrich or me, all the lands and gold should pass to Ulrich's daughter, only if she prove to be a spotless woman.

CONRAD. Spotless women are hard to find.

LORD. *You're* telling *me?*

WIFE. We prayed fervently for a son but the prayer was in vain.

LORD. You were born to us. I . . .

WIFE. He was in despair.

LORD. I was in despair because I saw the land, the gold, the prestige slipping from my grasp.

WIFE. You couldn't live with him. Cursing, restless, cruel to the servants.

LORD. But hold, I said when you were born, all is not lost.

WIFE. He got a scheme.

LORD. I'm a brilliant man. See you were born at midnight. Only the nurse and six waiting women knew your sex.

CONRAD. What happened to them?

LORD. I hanged everyone of them before an hour passed.

WIFE. Deep down he's a good man, but he had problems.

LORD. Next morning, all the barony went mad with rejoicing when I proclaimed a *son* was born—an heir to mighty Brandenburgh.

WIFE. See Ulrich had no children at all until . . .

LORD. When you were 10 years old a daughter was born to Ulrich.

CONRAD. Sure. Constantine.

WIFE. We grieved. Oh, how we grieved.

LORD. We hoped for measles, small pox, physicians, or other natural enemies of infancy, but she lived. But it is nothing. We are safe. We have a son and is not our son the future Duke? You, Conrad, will be that future Duke.

Conrad. So that's why all these years this secret had to be . . .

Wife. Yes.

Lord. Sorry. But we are grateful that you kept that secret, Conrad.

Conrad. Oh, I kept it. All the other nobles' sons wonder why I'm no good at polo, but the secret is kept.

Lord. We tell you all this now because age is upon my brother Ulrich. He's feeble. Cares of state tax him. He wants you to come to Brandenburgh and be as Duke in act not yet in name. You leave tonight.

Wife. Remember well Conrad—a warning now— There's a law as old as Germany that if any woman sit for a single instant on the throne before she has been absolutely crowned—she shall be put to death.

Lord. Pronounce your judgments from the Premier's chair which stands at the foot of the throne. Do this until you are crowned and safe.

Wife. It is not likely that your sex will be discovered. But still wisdom demands to make all things safe as you can in this treacherous earthly life.

Lord. What is it my knight daughter?

Conrad. Oh, my parents. Is it for this that my life hath been a lie? Was it only that I might cheat my cousin Constance of her rights? Spare me from this; I beg you.

Lord. I hanged a nurse, Conrad.

Wife. And six ladies in waiting.

Lord. All good help. And you, hussy, are worried about your cousin Constance's rights?

Conrad. Spare me.

LORD. I will not spare thee. Be gone to the Dukes instantly. I don't want to hear another word.

(CONRAD *bows and exits.*)

LORD. The gratitude for all I've done!

WIFE. Dearest.

LORD. Just the money I paid the shrewd and handsome Count Detzin to go to Brandenburgh to be Satan himself with the up till now pure Constance. Worry. Worry. Worry. Worry. Worry. Worry.

WIFE. Trust me in this matter. Count Detzin could sway any woman. Those eyes. Rest, my Lord. Leave bodings. All is well. Leave the owls to croak. To bed with ye, and dream of Brandenburgh and Grandeur. (*She helps him to exit.*)

LORD. Worry. Worry. Worry. Offspring! Why do we have them? Worry. Worry. Worry.

(*The* HERALD *enters from the other side of the stage. He blows his trumpet. He changes the banner behind the throne to read "Brandenburgh." He moves the smaller throne forward.*)

HERALD. Part II. Festivity in Brandenburgh.

(*Cheering and trumpets are heard off stage.* LADY CONSTANCE *enters crying. A servant follows. He may be played by the* HERALD.)

SERVANT. Lady Constance, Conrad is entering the City. You must join your mother and father in greeting him.

CONSTANCE. I don't care.

SERVANT. But Lady Constance.

CONSTANCE. I said I don't care. The Villin Detzin is gone—fled. I loved him. I dared to love a man with those eyes even though I knew the Duke, my father, would never let me wed him. I am lost. I am so lost. (*Sounds outside become louder. Lights fade as* CONSTANCE *goes on sobbing.*) Those blue eyes!

(*Lights come up.* HERALD *enters and speaks while* CONRAD *sits on the smaller throne. The* DUKE *in the larger, and* LADY CONSTANCE *stands by her father.*)

HERALD. Part III. Pay attention. Here's where the plot thickens.

CONRAD. (*A peasant stands before him.*) . . . and because your wife was lost in the landslide and you have been loyal to my uncle all these years, we shall provide you with another wife. (CONRAD *snaps his fingers. A beautiful servant woman comes out and goes to the peasant.*)

PEASANT. Oh, thank you. Oh, God, thank you. You are the heir to all that is good. She more than replaces Ilka. (*He takes his woman and they go off giggling.*)

CONSTANCE. He is so just, Father, so generous.

DUKE. Yes. You've been gaining a lot of weight, Constance. (*She tries to pull in her stomach.*) I think you need to be chased around the castle more. (*He laughs.*)

SERVANT. (*To* CONRAD.) Here is the next case, my Liege.

DUKE. Enough, he has had enough today. Forty-three decisions in one day is enough for our young Solomon. (*The* DUKE *rises. The* SERVANT *leaves.*) Conrad, you have won the loyalty of our kingdom. You will be a compassionate, just and wise ruler. If I still had my own teeth, I'd help you more. I will go nap now, Constance.

CONRAD. Thank you and good day, Uncle. (SERVANT *helps the* DUKE *leave the stage.*)

CONSTANCE. (*As* CONRAD *looks at her and tries to sneak off.*) Why do you do this?

CONRAD. Do what, Constance?

CONSTANCE. Avoid me? What have I done? Over the months we've become such good friends and now—

CONRAD. You have done nothing. It's . . . It's . . .

CONSTANCE. Conrad, pity a tortured heart. I love you, Conrad.

CONRAD. But . . . (*She throws her arms around* CONRAD.)

CONSTANCE. The pity you took when you first came. The hours of talks that calmed my tortured heart. You do love me. You must love me.

CONRAD. Constance, I . . . please . . . I . . .

CONSTANCE. Say you'll be my own, Conrad.

CONRAD. (*Fighting her off now.*) You know not what you ask. It is forever impossible. (CONRAD *runs off stage.* CONSTANCE *starts to go after, but stops and begins to cry.*)

CONSTANCE. To think that he was despising my love at the very moment that I thought it was melting his cruel heart. I hate you now, Conrad. He spurned me like a dog! Me! (*She runs off in the other direction as the* HERALD *comes back out.*)

HERALD. (*As he changes the banner from Bradenburgh back to Klugenstien and moves the small throne chair back.*) Part IV—The Revelation. The drama. The excitement. I only hope and pray it gets more risque. God, let it get more risque. Just this once and I'll never ask for anything else. (*Exit.*)

*(The LORD of Klugenstien takes the throne. He is
    snoring in a deep sleep. His wife enters.)*

WIFE. My husband, wake. The Lady Constance.

LORD. Huh! Huh!

WIFE. The Lady Constance. We must go to the trial.

LORD. What is it? Oh, it's you. I mistook you for a
concubine, I'm sorry.

WIFE. The Lady Constance has given birth to a
child out of wedlock.

LORD. Ah ha. Long live Duke Conrad. For lo his
crown is assured from this day forward anyway one
looks at it.

WIFE. That devil Detzin did his errand well. He
shall be rewarded handsomely.

LORD. It's those eyes.

*(The lights dim. The HERALD runs out and changes the
    banner back to Brandenburg and again moves the
    smaller throne downstage away from the larger.
    The lights come up again full.)*

HERALD. Part V. Sit closer together. This is the awful catastrophe. I'm sorry I prayed so hard.

*(Several Barons and Lords sit around the stage in-
    cluding the Lord Klugenstien. CONRAD clad in an
    ermine cloak sits on the small throne. The old
    DUKE sits in the larger.)*

DUKE. Nobles, Barons of the realm. You are here to
bear witness to the trial of a crime.

*(The Lady of Klugenstien sneaks in and quickly takes
    her place beside her husband, the LORD. She is
    disheveled.)*

LORD. Has Count Ditzen been rewarded?

WIFE. Most generously.

DUKE. You know what has transpired. My daughter has displeased me. So let her trial begin.

CONRAD. I ask the Duke publicly. I beg the Duke once more, please do not let me be the one to sit in judgment.

DUKE. No one is wiser than you. She has broken my heart. Only you can mete out what is truly fair. I say let it begin!

(*Trumpets blare off stage. One of the Barons acts as* CHIEF LORD.)

CHIEF LORD. Prisoner, stand forth.

(CONSTANCE *enters and stands in a witness box.*)

CHIEF LORD. Most noble lady, before the great judge of this realm it hath been charged and proven that out of holy wedlock your grace hath given birth unto a child and by ancient law, the penalty is death excepting in one sole contingency, where of his grace, the Acting Duke, Lord Conrad, will advise you in his solemn sensitive manner.

WIFE. Those eyes. They knock a lady right off her . . .

LORD. Shhhhhhh!

CONRAD. (*Rises.*) Noble followers of . . .

DUKE. (*He rises and* CONRAD *stops speaking.*) Not there, Lord Conrad, not there. It is not lawful to judge upon any royal life except from the throne itself.

(*Barons all buzz and nod approval.*)

CONRAD. But I'm not crowned.

LORD. Worry. Worry. Worry. Worry. Worry.

DUKE. It is all right. Only an uncrowned *woman* may not sit upon the royal throne under pain of death. (CONRAD *looks around nervously as the Barons again nod and buzz that the old* DUKE *is right.*) Well?

(*The crowd begins to mumble why do you hesitate?* CONRAD *walks up to the throne and sits without touching the chair. The* DUKE *pushes him down.*)

CONRAD. Oh, yes. Thank you.

LORD. (*To wife.*) A nurse and 6 ladies in waiting. Worry. Worry. Worry.

CONRAD. Prisoner, In . . . In . . . In the name of our sovereign Lord Ulrich, Duke of Brandenburgh, I proceed to my solemn duty. The ancient law says except you produce the partner of your guilt and deliver him up to the execution, you must surely die. Save yourself. I emplore you. Name the father of the child.

(*Pause. Silence.* CONSTANCE *looks around; then she looks back at* CONRAD.)

CONSTANCE. Thou. Thou art the man!

(*General consternation.* CONRAD'S *mother swoons.*)

DUKE. (*As guards grab* CONRAD.) If you lie, Constance, you will die.

CONSTANCE. It is no lie, Father.

LORD. Unhand him!

CONRAD. I swear on my mother's grave.

LORD. Which might not be too far off, if you don't unhand him.

CONSTANCE. He said he loved me but he just wanted to cast rocks into the ocean.

DUKE. I cannot believe it.

LORD. *You* cannot believe it?

DUKE. Have you, Conrad, anything to say?

WIFE. The rouse is up. The truth is . . .

CONRAD. The truth is . . . if Constance will have me, I will marry her.

LORD. Huh?

DUKE. Then it was true.

CONSTANCE. Oh, Father please, he is too young for the execution's blade. (*General cheering and agreement with* CONSTANCE.) Please, please, please, oh please. (CONSTANCE *kisses her father.*)

DUKE. So be it. The marriage ceremony will begin immediately. All rejoice the joining of the House of Klugenstien and the House of Brandenburgh.

LORD. A nurse and 6 ladies in waiting.

WIFE. They're actually going to be married. (*She faints in her husband's arms again.*)

DUKE. Women. Let us all have some wine and music. Music.

(CONRAD *and* CONSTANCE, *hand in hand, cross downstage as the wine is poured and the Medieval music begins.*)

CONSTANCE. Don't be angry Conrad; we're going to be so happy. Dance with me. (*They begin to dance.*) Will you be happy, Conrad?

CONRAD. If I could only tell you. Rejoice. Go ahead Look at them. Rejoicing.

CONSTANCE. Forgive me for lying, Conrad, I love you that much.

CONRAD. When the wedding night comes around, remind me to tell you something.

CONSTANCE. Will it make me happy?

CONRAD. You could get a laugh out of it.

CONSTANCE. How funny is it?

CONRAD. It's going to keep you in stitches for 50–60 years.

CONSTANCE. (*Laughs.*) Oh, Conrad you're so funny. That's it. From now on we'll laugh, laugh, laugh, do nothing but laugh.

(*The music swells as* CONRAD *and* CONSTANCE *dance around the stage to the approval of all and the lights fade.*)

HERALD. (*Before lights fade completely.*) No one will dispute Constance on that final point. Just a footnote to the curious. Constance and Conrad lived happily ever after until one year when Constance's husband became pregnant by a certain Count Detzin. They were all hanged and the kingdom is still in probate court.

PROPERTY PLOT

2 chairs; one preferably a wooden arm chair and the 2nd a smaller chair

several colorful banners (optional)

1 banner which reads Klugenstien on one side and Brandenburgh on the other

a pitcher of wine and goblets

COSTUME PLOT

1 herald's costume

1 knight's outfit

1 long robe and crown for Lord of Klugenstien

1 long robe and crown for Duke of Brandenburgh

1 long gown for Conrad's mother

1 long gown for Constance

1 peasant's costume female

1 peasant's costume male

1 servant's outfit

1 ermine cloak for Conrad

1 tunic for the Chief Lord

NOTE: Only Conrad need really be attired as a Medieval Knight. The others may simply wear robes or long dresses, or the production may be done with all characters dressed in black with a few handmade wire crowns for the Lord and Duke.

73

Other Publications for Your Interest

VIVIEN
(COMIC DRAMA)
By PERCY GRANGER

2 men, 1 woman—Unit set

Recently staged to acclaim at Lincoln Center, this lovely piece is about a young stage director who visits his long-lost father in a nursing home and takes him to see a production of "The Seagull" that he staged. Along the way, each reveals a substantial truth about himself, and the journey eventually reaches its zenith in a restaurant after the performance. "A revealing father-son portrait that gives additional certification to the author's position as a very original playwright."—N.Y. Times. "The dialogue has the accuracy of real people talking."—N.Y. Post

---

LANDSCAPE WITH WAITRESS
(COMEDY)
By ROBERT PINE

1 man, 1 woman—Interior

Arthur Granger is an unsuccessful novelist who lives a Walter Mitty-like fantasy existence. Tonight, he is dining out in an Italian restaurant which seems to have only one waitress and one customer—himself. As Arthur selects his dinner he has fantasies of romantic conquest, which he confides to the audience and to his notebook. While Arthur's fantasies take him into far-fetched plots, the waitress acts out the various characters in his fantasy. Soon, Arthur is chattering and dreaming away at such a quick clip that neither he nor we can be entirely sure of his sanity. Arthur finishes his dinner and goes home, ending as he began—as a lover *manqué*. "...a landscape of the mind."—Other Stages. "... has moments of true originality and a bizarre sense of humor...a devious and slightly demented half-hour of comedy."—N.Y. Times. Recently a hit at New York's excellent Ensemble Studio Theatre.

Other Publications for Your Interest

MOVIE OF THE MONTH
(COMEDY)
By DANIEL MELTZER

2 men—Interior

This new comedy by the author of the ever-popular *The Square Root of Love* is an amusing satire of commercial television. B.S., a TV programming executive, is anxious to bolster his network's ratings, which have been sagging of late due to programming disasters such as a documentary called "The Ugly Truth" (says B.S.: "What the hell is The Ugly Truth, and how the hell did it get into our Prime Time?") His eagerbeaver assistant, appropriately named Broun, has found a script which he is sure can be made into a hit "Movie of the Month". It's about this Danish prince, see, who comes home from college to find that his uncle has murdered his father and married his mother . . . Well, naturally, B.S. has his own ideas about how to fix such a totally unbelievable plot . . .   (#17621)

SUNDANCE
(ALL GROUPS—COMEDY)
By MEIR Z. RIBALOW

5 men—Simple interior

This new comedy from the author of *Shrunken Heads* is set in a sort of metaphysical wild west saloon. The characters include Hickock, Jesse, the Kid, and the inevitable Barkeep. Hickock kills to uphold the law. Jesse kills for pleasure. The Kid kills to bring down The Establishment. What if, wonders the Barkeep, they met up with the Ultimate Killer—who kills for no reason, who kills simply because that's what he does? Enter Sundance. He does not kill to uphold the law, for pleasure, or to make a political statement, or because he had a deprived childhood. And he proceeds to kill everyone, exiting at the end with his sixguns blazing! "Witty, strong, precise, unusually well-written."—The Guardian. "A brilliant piece."—Dublin Evening Press. This co-winner of the 1981 Annual NYC Metropolitan Short Play Festival has been a success in 6 countries!   (#3113)

Other Publications for Your Interest

A GALWAY GIRL
(ALL GROUPS—DRAMA)
By GERALDINE ARON

1 man, 1 woman—Interior

A married couple, seated at opposite ends of a table, reminisce about their life together. Each presents the situation from his or her point of view, rarely addressing each other directly. The characters are young to begin with, then middle-aged, then old, then one of them dies. The anecdotes they relate are both humorous and tragic. Their lives seem wasted, yet at the end the wife's muted gesture of affection conveys the love that can endure through years of household bickering and incompatibility. A critical success in London, Ireland and the author's native South Africa. "A very remarkable play."—Times Literary Supplement, London. "A touching account of two wasted lives."—Daily Telegraph, London. "A minute tapestry cross-stitched with rich detail—invested with a strong strain of uncomfortable truths."—The Irish Times, Dublin.

TWO PART HARMONY
(PLAY)
By KATHARINE LONG

1 man, 1 woman—Interior

A play about a confrontation of wits between an alert, pre-adolescent girl and a mentally unsettled child-man. On a spring morning in 1959, eight year old Jessie Corington, home alone on a sick day from school, receives an unexpected visit from Hank Everett, a former friend of the family who used to look like Bobby Darin. From the moment he arrives, Hank's eccentric behavior challenges Jessie's cherished belief in adult maturity. Gradually, however, she welcomes her new found playmate and becomes entranced as he enlists her aid in a telephone search for his estranged wife. As the play builds, their bond of friendship is almost shattered when the violence beneath Hank's innocence surfaces against his will. "The work of an artist skilled in deft, understated draughtmanship."—Village Voice.

Other Publications for Your Interest

NOW THERE'S JUST THE THREE OF US

(COMEDY)

By MICHAEL WELLER

4 men, 1 woman—Interior

Perry and Frank are roommates. Perry greatly envies Frank's expertise with the ladies, which he knows all about because Frank has told him. Well: enter one Deke. Neither Perry nor Frank knows Deke; but he convinces each that he is a good friend of the other and proceeds to move in. Deke is a *real* ladies' man. He brings his girlfriend in, too and they move into the bedroom, displacing Frank. When a mysterious man from "the agency" comes looking for Deke, he splits, leaving his girlfriend behind with Frank and Perry. She announces that she has decided to devote herself to sex, and Frank and Perry's eyes get bigger than saucers as they realize now, there's just the three of them! Premiered in London and has had many worldwide productions. An excellent choice for colleges by the author of *Moonchildren* and *Loose Ends*.   (#16638)

THE TANGLED SNARL

(COMEDY)

By JOHN RUSTAN & FRANK SEMERANO

3 men, 2 women, 1 boy—Interior

To Private Detective Spuds Idaho, life in L.A. is ". . . a 24 furlong race around a track made of quicksand." When the dying Legs Flamingo leaves him a package to deliver, Spuds gets curious. Why is Leslie Detweiler more interested in the package than in the death of her husband: "Excuse me, but you look pretty collected for a lady whose breadwinner just got sliced four ways." Why was Legs mixed up with mob figure, Vito "Fingers" Scampi: "So Fingers had Legs under his thumb." And how did it figure in with the Krieger heist: "The Commissioner was embarrassed. His boys in blue were red in the face." With the aid of his secretary, Ginny, and a wise-cracking little kid, it all untangles for Spuds Idaho.   (#22616)

Bible Herstory

PATRICIA MONTLEY

(May Double.) Satire.

18 females—Bare Stage

Bible Herstory, a one-act feminist satire in six scenes featuring an all-woman cast. In "Paradise Abandoned," Eve convinces God not to stifle Her creativity just because She made a mistake in creating Adam. In "Noah's Ark-itect," Noah's wife and daughter prepare for the flood and "inspire" Noah to build a boat. "The Sacrifice of Sarah" shows Abraham's wife working on a theatrical project to save a lazy Isaac's life. In "Miriam in Labor," Moses' sister bargains with Pharaoh's daughter for better working conditions. In "Queen Solomon and the Paternity Suit," her Majesty proposes to cut in half a philandering charioteer claimed by both wife and mistress. In "The Renunciation," Mary rejects the Angel Gabriella's offer of the saviorship of the world, but agrees to have a son.

———————◆———————

Out of Our Father's House

Play with music. (All Groups.)

BASED ON EVE MERRIAM'S
Growing Up Female in America: Ten Lives

3 females play 6 roles
Musicians—1 Interior

Arranged for the stage by Paula Wagner, Jack Hofsiss and Eve Merriam. Music by Ruth Cawford Seeger adapted by Daniel Schrier. With additional music by Daniel Shrier and Marjorie Lipari.

Taken entirely from diaries, journals and letters of the characters portrayed. They are a schoolgirl—founder of the Women's Suffrage Movement, an astronomer, a labor organizer, a minister, a doctor and a woman coming out of the Jewish ghetto. They are watched as they grow up, marry and bear children. They do not covet men's jobs, but when they want careers they are ostracized. A very moving play seen through the words and eyes of 19th century American women. Write for information about music.

HERE'S HOW

A Basic Stagecraft Book

**THOROUGHLY REVISED
AND ENLARGED**

by HERBERT V. HAKE

COVERING 59 topics on the essentials of stagecraft (13 of them brand new). *Here's How* meets a very real need in the educational theater. It gives to directors and others concerned with the technical aspects of play production a complete and graphic explanation of ways of handling fundamental stagecraft problems.

The book is exceptional on several counts. It not only treats every topic thoroughly, but does so in an easy-to-read style every layman can understand. Most important, it is prepared in such a way that for every topic there is a facing page of illustrations (original drawings and photographs)—thus giving the reader a complete graphic presentation of the topic along with the textual description of the topic.

Because of the large type, the large size of the pages (9″ x 12″), and the flexible metal binding, *Here's How* will lie flat when opened and can be laid on a workbench for a director to read while in a *standing* position.